For Joseph & Jea

THE PIG WHO DIDN'T WANT TO GET DIRTY!

by

PARIS & TAYLOR™

Standing on a barn, in front of the rising sun,
A Rooster cries out, “A *new* day has begun!”

Soon, the animals begin to move to and fro.

Waking up, they *welcome* the sun's glow.

With it, comes the start of a *new* day.

They can let their children out to play.

The children are full of energy and fun.
They'll *play* until the moon replaces the sun!

The baby chicks play chase in the farm's *dusty* yard!

Wrestling in a corral, the young bulls are playing *hard*!
Yeooow!

Rolling in the straw are the baby sheep.
Soon they will be tired and fall asleep.
Baaa
Ba-HaHa
PLOP!

The piglets *love* to wallow in a *muddy* pit.
For them there is *nothing* quite like it!

But one piglet *hated* getting dirty.
This guy was *clean* as could be!

He was a pig who *hated* grime and dust!

Keeping his pink skin *clean* was a must!

His name was Squeaky, but *everyone* called him "Squeaky-Clean!"

Everyone *teased* him and said things that were mean!

But Squeaky *never* paid them much mind at all.

He kept his head up and *always* walked tall!

Squeaky's pop *wasn't* happy with his boy.

Watching him, his heart was *not* full of joy!

"He *won't* get dirty!" he moaned to his wife.

"How can a pig lead a *dirt-free* life?"

"Accept him," Squeaky's mom said, "for who he is.
So what if he *doesn't* want to get dirty. Gee whiz!"
But Squeaky's father continued to plan and plot,
Accepting his son hated *dirt*, he could not!

"I think I've got it," he said. "Yes, I'm sure!
It isn't anything a mud bath *wouldn't* cure!"

"It'll feel *strange* when the mud *oozes* up to his nose!"

"But soon, it will *uncurl* his tail and *tickle* his toes!"

"He'll love it *so* much," Squeaky's father said with a shout,
"To get him to leave, we'll need dynamite to *blast* him out!"

"A *sillier* thing," our pal's mom said, "I *never* heard.
Don't say a *thing* to him about a *mud bath*. Not a word.
He may be different *but* he's happy. That is *easy* to see.
One day you'll be *proud* of him, just like me!"

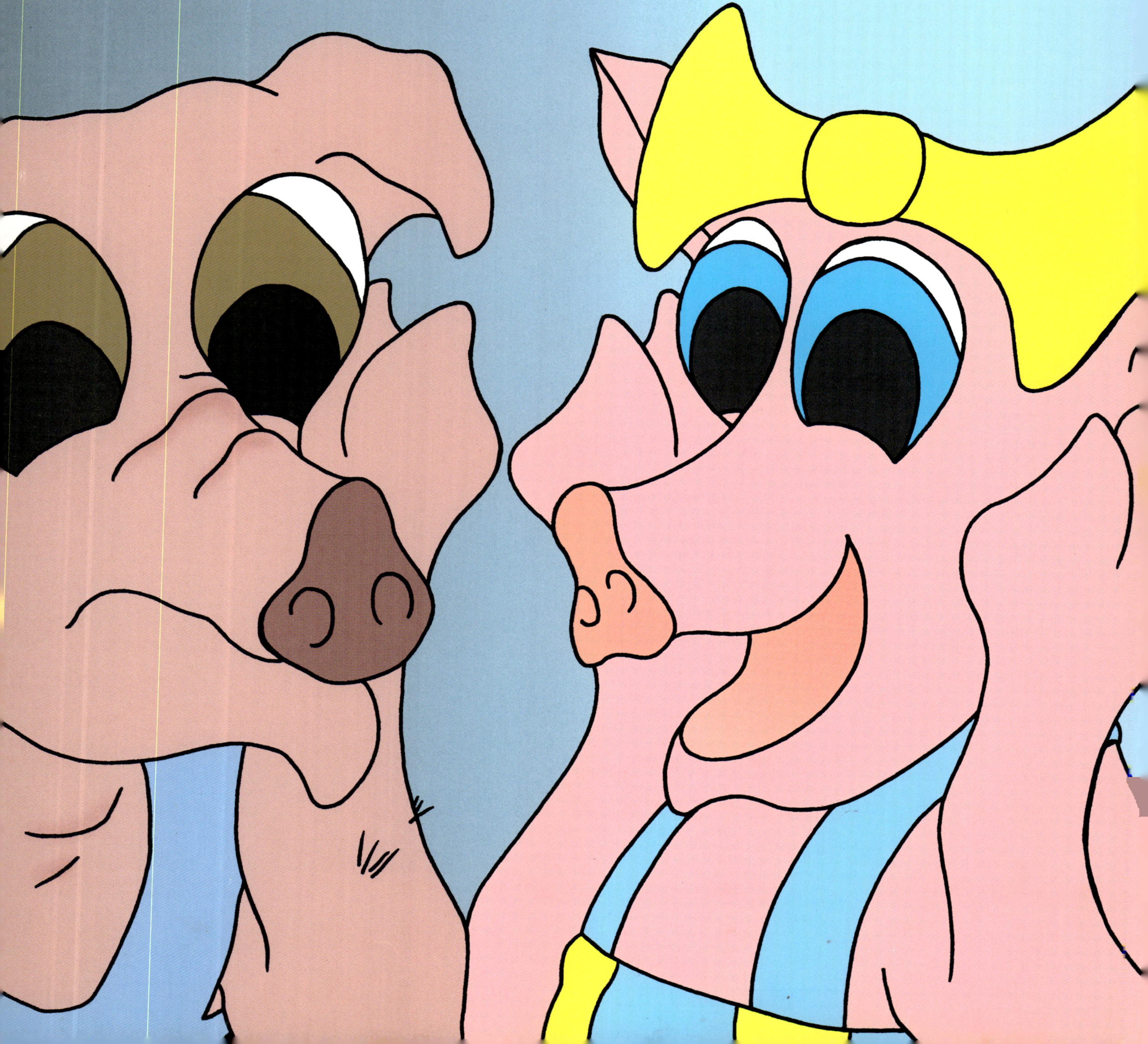

In the barnyard, there were lots of *wonders* to be found!
Squeaky was walking slowly, catching *every* sight and sound.
He found the *dusty* yard where the chicks were playing chase...

Deciding to watch them, he took a seat in a *clean* place.

The chicks noticed the pig *enjoying* their game.
One of them asked if he'd *like* to do the same.
"Just sitting there watching *can't* be fun at all.
Why not join us? I'm sure you'd have a ball!"

"I'd love to," Squeaky said. "It looks like fun.
But my feet would be *dirty* when I'd be done!"

"And my bath isn't until later. It's not until seven-ten.
I just *couldn't* walk around with *dirty* feet until then!"

"When does *his* kind make cleanliness a habit?

A *clean* pig," a chick said, "is like a *slow* rabbit!"

They *teased* Squeaky! Then they *teased* him some more!

But it *didn't* bother him. He left to find *other* places to explore.

Soon, Squeaky came upon the grassy corral.
The bulls were wrestling, each against a pal!
Spotting him, one looked the piglet's way
And asked our pal if he would like to play.

"Join us," he said. "I'm *sure* you'll be amused!"

Instead, our pal Squeaky *politely* refused.

"Playing in that field would be fun," he said. "There's *no* doubt.
But I'd be *covered* with grass stains and they're *hard* to get out!
Thanks for asking but I'm afraid I'll *have* to pass."

"A *pig*," laughed the bull, "who's *afraid* to play in the grass!"

The bulls enjoyed a laugh at Squeaky's expense!

Our pal just moved away from the corral's fence.

Squeaky heard laughter from behind a door.
The pig trotted in. He *wanted* to see more!

The sheep were rolling in the straw and hay.
One asked Squeaky if he wanted to play.

"Join us in the hay," one laughed. "Jump on in!
You'll have a *great* time!" he said with a grin.

Squeaky *didn't* want to jump into that straw heap.
And he *didn't* want to offend any of the sheep.

"I can't," Squeaky said. "And *don't* think I'm being mean.
But I'd be *covered* with straw and have to pick myself clean!"

The sheep teased him until they heard a voice that was kind.

"Leave him be," it said. "A *handsomer* pig, you'll *never* find!"

The voice belonged to Mr. Jones, the *owner* of the farm.

Reaching down, he *scooped* Squeaky up with an arm.

Looking at the piglet, he scratched his chin.
"Squeaky," he said, "you're a *cinch* to win!"

"I *don't* understand," our pal stated with a smile on his face.
"You will," Mr. Jones said. "I'm taking you to a *special* place!"

The news Squeaky was going somewhere "*special*" traveled quick!

Squeaky was the *only* animal the farmer happened to pick.

Mr. Jones and the pig left in a pick-up truck.

Squeaky's mom was there to *wish* her son luck.

They reached a place with *excitement* in the air.

This place was the annual county fair!

Soon, Squeaky was as *proud* as could be.

He was on display for *everyone* to see!

Squeaky won *first* place and got a *blue* ribbon.

If I said there was a *handsomer* pig, I'd be fibbin'!

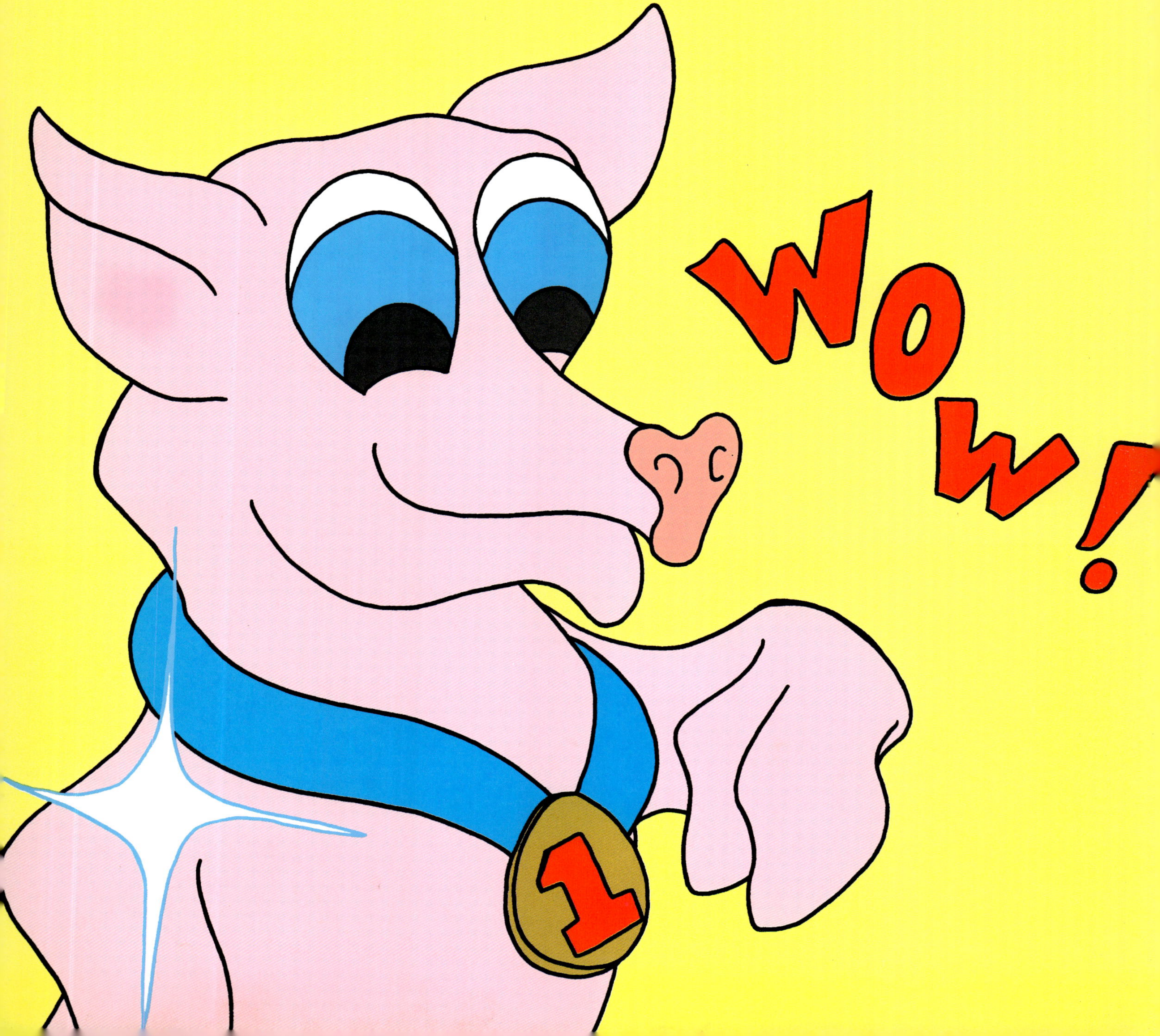

Squeaky returned and brought the news of his *big* day!

With that news *everyone* saw him in a *different* way!

Instead of teasing him, they *praised* him out loud!
All of the other animals were *now* very proud!
No one was *prouder* of Squeaky than his mother,
Unless you looked, then you *might* find one other.

Just as Squeaky's mom had said he'd be,
Squeaky's pop was as *proud* of him as she!

Squeaky the pig proved that being different *wasn't* wrong.

Different is *just* different. It *doesn't* mean you *don't* belong!

Everyone fits in somewhere. *Everyone* has a *special* place.

When you're teased, walk away with a smile on your face.

SPECIAL ANNOUNCEMENT!
Pressure!
Pressure!
If you think I was *teased* and *picked on* wait until you read my friend Lenny's book!

THE LEMMING WHO DIDN'T WANT TO TAKE THE PLUNGE!
BOOK # 12
Collect Them All!
by PARIS & TAYLOR™
Wow!
These guys look mean!

CHECK LIST PAGE!

Check off the book you have!

Visit our web site at: www.parisandtaylor.com

- ☐ THE ELEPHANT WHO COULDN'T REMEMBER!
- ☐ THE TURTLE WHO FELT BOXED IN!
- ☐ THE BIRD WHO DIDN'T WANT TO FLY SOUTH FOR THE WINTER!
- ☐ THE BIRD WHO WAS AFRAID TO CLEAN THE CROCODILE'S TEETH!
- ☐ THE BEAR WHO COULDN'T HIBERNATE! (SLEEP)
- ☐ THE STRAW THAT DIDN'T BREAK THE CAMEL'S BACK!
- ☐ THE SKUNK WHO DIDN'T WANT TO STINK!
- ☐ THE OPOSSUM WHO DIDN'T WANT TO PLAY DEAD ANYMORE!
- ☐ THE PENGUIN WHO HATED THE COLD BECAUSE HE WAS ALL DRESSED UP AND HAD NO PLACE TO GO!
- ☐ THE ROOSTER WHO DIDN'T WANT TO WAKE UP EARLY ANYMORE!
- ☑ THE PIG WHO DIDN'T WANT TO GET DIRTY!
- ☐ THE LEMMING WHO DIDN'T WANT TO TAKE THE PLUNGE!
- ☐ THE FISH WHO COULDN'T SWIM!
- ☐ THE HYENA WHO WOULDN'T LAUGH!
- ☐ THE BIRD WHO WAS AFRAID OF HEIGHTS!
- ☐ THE EAGLE WHO DIDN'T WANT TO WEAR HIS GLASSES ANYMORE!
- ☐ AND MORE!